The Mystical Element in Judaism

Abraham J. Heschel

The Mystical Element In Judaism

Introduction
by Reuven Kimelman

This essay has been first published in Louis Finkelstein,
"The Jews, Their History, Culture and Religion".
2 vols., Harpers, 1949, New York.

Published here with permission of Prof. Finkelstein's estate,
all proceeds go to The Jewish Theological Seminary Press.

ISBN 1-59045-917-2

CONTENTS

Introduction by Reuven Kimelman v

1. The Meaning of Jewish Mysticism 1
2. The Exaltation of Man 7
3. The En Sof and his Manifestations 13
4. The Doctrine of the Shekinah 19
5. Mystic Experience 25
6. The Torah – A Mystic Reality 31
7. The Mystic Way of Life 37
8. The Concern for God 45

Notes 51
Bibliography 57

Introduction

by Reuven Kimelman

"*The Mystical Element in Judaism*," is Abraham Joshua Heschel's alternative to Gershom Scholem's thesis of Kabbalah as significantly a gnostic phenomenon.* Scholem's *Major Trends in Jewish Mysticism* was published in New York in 1941; Heschel's essay was completed four years later, albeit published in 1949. Heschel finished his essay at the age of 38. Scholem delivered the lecture behind his essay in 1938 at the age of 41. In 1944, Heschel reviewed Scholem's book in *The Journal of Religion* and then wrote in "Al Ruach HaQodesh Bimei Beinayim," that "they still have not evaluated properly the place of mystical experience in Jewish life." In the first week of 1945, Heschel lectured at YIVO in Yiddish on "The East European Era in Jewish History" which became the basis of *The Earth Is the Lord's*, finished in 1948. His discussion of Kabbalah there, minus the quotations, is from "The Mystical Element in Judaism." Thus already in 1944 Heschel was involved in revising Scholem's thesis as attested to by his essays on medieval religious experience and "The Mystical Element in Judaism," all composed in the 1940's.

Comparing Heschel's essay with Scholem's "The Zohar II: The Theosophic Doctrine" in his Major Trends pinpoints their disagreement. Illustrative of this difference is their reason for

---

* For an expansion of this thesis, see Reuven Kimelman, "Abraham Joshua Heschel's Theology of Judaism and The Rewriting of Jewish Intellectual History," *Journal of Jewish Thought and Philosophy* 17 (2009), pp. 207–38.

referring to J. Abelson's *The Immanence of God in Rabbinical Literature*. Scholem cites Abelson to illustrate the difference between Zoharic and Rabbinic conceptions of the Shekhinah. By focusing on the difference, Scholem disassociates the Zoharic understanding from its Rabbinic antecedents and aligns it with gnostic sources, pagan mythology, and post-Lurianic writings. By making his next chapter, "Isaac Luria and his School," Scholem implies the validity of the Lurianic reading of the Zohar. In contrast, in the section, "The Doctrine of the Shekhinah," Heschel footnotes Abelson to underscore the link between Zoharic and Rabbinic conceptions. His citations are almost all Zoharic without a single Lurianic source. As opposed to any Lurianic, gnostic, neoplatonic negation of concrete reality, he defines the Kabbalistic as one whose "living with the infinite does not make him alien to the finite."

Scholem cites gnostic sources to establish the theosophic link; Heschel cites midrashic ones to establish the rabbinic link, namely, the paradoxical idea "that not only is God necessary to man but that man is also necessary to God, to the unfolding of His plans in this world." The two topics that lack any correspondence to Scholem's chapter are Heschel's second section, "The Exaltation of Man," and the seventh section, "The Mystic Way of Life." In the former, he argues that "the belief in the greatness of man, in the metaphysical effectiveness of his physical acts, is an ancient motif of Jewish thinking." In the latter, he underscores the primacy of prayer and worship. Save for the discussions of the Ein Sof and the *Sefirot*, the differences exceed the commonality. Most of the Zoharic sources cited by Heschel do not even appear in Scholem's essay. This more balanced treatment corrects Scholem's proclivity for the theosophic.

Recent research has vindicated Heschel's focus on the dynamics of the religious life and on the foundations of Kabbalistic thought in classical Jewish thinking. The change that Heschel initiated in assessing Kabbalah's intellectual roots is part of a trend in recent scholarship highlighting continuities over discontinuities. The perception of discontinuities in historical research is frequently due to the lack of data. As data grows so grows the perception of continuities. In Heschel's case, however, it was not so much the discovery of new data as the reconceptualizing of old data that made him the trendsetter in disclosing the links between the Biblical and the Rabbinic, the Rabbinic and the Kabbalistic, the Kabbalistic and the Hasidic.

Reuven Kimelman

THE MEANING OF JEWISH MYSTICISM

1

There are people who take great care to keep away from the mists produced by fads and phrases. They refuse to convert realities into opinions, mysteries into dogmas, and ideas into a multitude of words, for they realize that all concepts are but glittering motes in a sunbeam. They want to see the sun itself. Confined to our study rooms, our knowledge seems to us a pillar of light j but when we stand at the door that opens out to the Infinite, we see how insubstantial is our knowledge. Even when we shut the door to the Infinite and retire to the narrow limits of notions our minds cannot remain confined. Again, to some people explanations and opinions are a token of wonder's departure, like a curfew after which they may not come abroad. In the cabbalists, the drive and the fire and the light are never put out.

Like the vital power in ourselves that gives us the ability to fight and to endure, to dare and to conquer, which drives us to experience the bitter and the perilous, there is an urge in wistful souls to starve rather than be fed on sham and distortion. To the cabbalists God is as real as life, and as nobody would be satisfied with mere knowing or reading about life, so they are not content to suppose or to prove logically that there is a God; they want to feel and to enjoy Him; not only to obey, but to approach Him.  They want to taste the whole wheat of spirit before it is ground by the millstones of reason. They would rather be overwhelmed by the symbols of the inconceivable than wield the definitions of the superficial.

Stirred by a yearning after the unattainable, they want to make the distant near, the abstract concrete, to transform the soul into a vessel for the transcendent, to grasp with the senses what is hidden from the mind, to express in symbols what the tongue cannot speak, what the reason cannot conceive, to experience as a reality what vaguely dawns in intuitions. "Wise is he who by the power of his own contemplation attains to the perception of the profound mysteries which cannot be expressed in words."[1]

The cabbalist is not content with being confined to what he is. His desire is not only to know more than what ordinary reason has to offer, but to be more than what he is; not only to comprehend the Beyond but to concur with it. He aims at the elevation and expansion of existence. Such expansion goes hand in hand with the exaltation of all being.

The universe, exposed to the violence of our analytical mind, is being broken apart. It is split into the known and unknown, into the seen and unseen. In mystic contemplation all things are seen as one.[2] The mystic mind tends to hold the world together: to behold the seen in conjunction with the unseen, to keep the fellowship with the unknown through the revolving door of the known, "to learn the higher supernal wisdom from all" that the Lord has created and to regain the knowledge that once was in the possession of men and "that has perished from them."[3] What our senses perceive is but the jutting edge of what is deeply hidden. Extending over into the invisible, the things of this world stand in a secret contact with that which no eye has ever perceived. Everything certifies to the sublime, the unapparent working jointly with the apparent. There is always a reverberation in the Beyond to every action here: "The Lord made this world corresponding to the world above, and everything which is above has its counterpart below … and yet they all constitute a unity",[4] "there being no object, however small, in this world, but what is subordinate to its counterpart above which has charge over it; and so whenever the thing below bestirs itself, there is a simultaneous stimulation of its counterpart above, as the two realms form one interconnected whole."[5]

Opposed to the idea that the world of perception is the bottom of reality, the mystics plunge into what is beneath the perceptible. What they attain in their quest is more than a vague impression or a spotty knowledge of the imperceptible. "Penetrating to the real essence of wisdom … they are resplendent with the radiance of supernal wisdom."[6] Their eyes perceive things of this world, while their hearts reverberate to the throbbing of the hidden. To them the secret is the core of the apparent; the known is but an aspect of the unknown. "All things below are symbols of that which is above."[7] They are sustained by the forces that flow from hidden worlds. There is no particular that is detached from universal meaning. What appears to be a center to the eye is but a point on the periphery around another center. Nothing here is final. The worldly is subservient to the otherworldly. You grasp the essence of the here by conceiving its beyond. For this world is the reality of the spirit in a state of trance. The manifestation of the mystery is partly suspended, with ourselves living in lethargy. Our normal consciousness is a state of stupor, in which our sensibility to the wholly real and our responsiveness to the stimuli of the spirit are reduced. The mystics, knowing that we are involved in a hidden history of the cosmos, endeavor to awake from the drowsiness and apathy and to regain the state of wakefulness for our enchanted souls.

It is a bold attitude of the soul, a steadfast quality of consciousness, that lends mystic character to a human being. A man who feels that he is closely enfolded by a power that is both lasting and holy will come to know that the spiritual is not an idea to which one can relate his will, but a realm which can even be affected by our deeds. What distinguishes the cabbalist is the attachment of his entire personality to a hidden spiritual realm. Intensifying this attachment by means of active devotion to it, by meditation upon its secrets, or even by perception of its reality, he becomes allied with the dynamics of hidden worlds. Sensitive to the imperceptible, he is stirred by its secret happenings.

Attachment to hidden worlds holds the cabbalist in the spell of things more basic than the things that dominate the interest of the common mind. The mystery is not beyond and away from us. It is our destiny. "The fate of the world depends upon the mystery."[7a] Our task is to adjust the details to the whole, the apparent to the hidden, the near to the distant. The passionate concern of the cabbalist for final goals endows him with the experience of surpassing all human limitations and powers. With all he is doing he is crossing the borders, breaking the surfaces, approaching the lasting sources of all things. Yet his living with the infinite does not make him alien to the finite.

The Exaltation of Man

2

In this exalted world man's position is unique. God has instilled in him something of Himself. Likeness to God is the essence of man. The Hebrew word for man, adam usually associated with the word for earth, *adamah*[8] was homiletically related by some cabbalists to the expression, "I will ascend above the heights of the clouds; I will be like (*eddamme*) the Most High" (Is. 14:14). Man's privilege is, as it were, to augment the Divine in the world, as it is said, "ascribe ye strength unto God" (Ps. 68:35).

Jewish mystics are inspired by a bold and dangerously paradoxical idea that not only is God necessary to man but that man is also necessary to God, to the unfolding of His plans in this world. Thoughts of this kind are indicated and even expressed in various Rabbinic sources. "When Israel performs the will of the Omnipresent, they add strength to the heavenly power; as it is said, 'To God we render strength!' " When, however, Israel does not perform the will of the Omnipresent, they weaken—if it is possible to say so—the great power of Him Who is above; as it is written "Thou didst weaken the Rock that begot thee"[9] (Deut. 32:18). In the *Zohar* this idea is formulated in a more specific way. Commenting on the passage in Ex. 17:8, "Then came Amalek and fought with Israel in Rephidim," R. Simeon said: "There is a deep allusion in the name 'Rephi-dim.' This war emanated from the attribute of Severe Judgment and it was a war above and a war below ... The Holy One, as it were, said: 'When Israel is worthy below, My power prevails in the universe; but when Israel is found to be unworthy, she weakens My power above, and the power of severe judgment predominates in the world.' So here, 'Amalek came and fought with Israel in Rephidim,' because the Israelites were 'weak' [in Hebrew: *raphe*, which the *Zohar* finds in the name 'Rephidim'] in the study of the Torah, as we have explained on another occasion."[10] Thus man's relationship to God should not be that of passive reliance upon His Omnipotence but that of active assistance. "The impious rely on their gods ... the righteous are the support of God."[11] The Patriarchs are therefore called "the chariot of the Lord."[12] The belief in the greatness of man, in the metaphysical effectiveness of his physical acts, is an ancient motif of Jewish thinking.

Man himself is a mystery. He is the symbol of all that exists. His life is the image of universal life. Everything was created in the spiritual image of the mystical man. "When the Holy One created man, He set in him all the images of the supernal mysteries of the world above, and all the images of the lower mysteries of the world below, and all are designed in man, who stands in the image of God."[13] Even the human body is full of symbolic significance. The skin, flesh, bones and sinews are but an outward covering, mere garments,[14] even though "the substances composing man's body belong to two worlds, namely, the world below and the world above."[15] The 248 limbs and 365 sinews are symbols of the 613 parts of the universe as well as of the 248 positive and 365 negative precepts of the Torah. Man's soul emanates from an upper region where it has a spiritual father and a spiritual mother, just as the body has a father and mother in this world.[16] The souls that abide in our bodies are a weak reflection of our upper souls, the seat of which is in heaven. Yet, though detached from that soul, we are capable of being in contact with it. When we pray we turn toward the upper soul as though we were to abandon the body and join our source.

Man is not detached from the realm of the unseen. He is wholly involved in it. Whether he is conscious of it or not, his actions are vital to all worlds, and affect the course of transcendent events. In a sense, by means of the Torah, man is the constant architect of the hidden universe. "This world was formed in the pattern of the world above, and whatever takes place in this earthly realm occurs also in the realm above."[17] One of the principles of the *Zohar* is that every move below calls forth a corresponding movement above.[18] Not only things, even periods of time are conceived as concrete entities. "Thus over every day below is appointed a day above, and a man should take heed not to impair that day. Now the act below stimulates a corresponding activity above. Thus if a man does kindness on earth, he awakens lovingkindness above, and it rests upon that day which is crowned therewith through him. Similarly, if he performs a deed of mercy, he crowns that day with mercy and it becomes his protector in the hour of need. So, too, if he performs a cruel action, he has a corresponding effect on that day and impairs it, so that subsequently it becomes cruel to him and tries to destroy him, giving him measure for measure."[19] Even what we consider potential is regarded as real and we may be held accountable for it: "…just as a man is punished for uttering an evil word, so is he punished for not uttering a good word when he had the opportunity, because he harms that speaking spirit which was prepared to speak above and below in holiness."[20]

The significance of great works done on earth is valued by their cosmic effects. Thus, *e.g.,* "When the first Temple was completed another Temple was erected at the same time, which was a center for all the worlds, shedding radiance upon all things and giving light to all the spheres. Then the worlds were firmly established, and all the supernal casements were opened to pour forth light, and all the worlds experienced such joys as had never been known to them before, and celestial and terrestrial beings alike broke forth in song. And the song which they sang is the Song of Songs."[21]

Endowed with metaphysical powers man's life is a most serious affair; "if a man's lips and tongue speak evil words, those words mount aloft and all proclaim 'keep away from the evil word of so-and-so, leave the path clear for the mighty serpent.' Then the holy soul leaves him and is not able to speak: it is in shame and distress, and is not given a place as before … Then many spirits bestir themselves, and one spirit comes down from that side and finds the man who uttered the evil word, and lights upon him and defiles him, and he becomes leprous."[22]

Man's life is full of peril. It can easily upset the balance and order of the universe. "A voice goes forth and proclaims: 'O ye people of the world, take heed unto yourselves, close the gates of sin, keep away from the perilous net before your feet are caught in it!' A certain wheel is ever whirling continuously round and round. Woe to those whose feet lose their hold on the wheel, for then they fall into the Deep which is predestined for the evildoers of the world! Woe to those who fall, never to rise and enjoy the light that is stored up for the righteous in the world to come!"[23]

The En Sof and His Manifestations

3

Mystic intuition occurs at an outpost of the mind, dangerously detached from the main substance of the intellect. Operating as it were in no-mind's land, its place is hard to name, its communications with critical thinking often difficult and uncertain and the accounts of its discoveries not easy to decode. In its main representatives, the cabbala teaches that man's life can be a rallying point of the forces that tend toward God, that this world is charged with His presence and every object is a cue to His qualities. To the cabbalist, God is not a concept, a generalization, but a most specific reality; his thinking about Him full of forceful directness. But He who is "the Soul of all souls"[24] is "the mystery of all mysteries." While the cabbalists speak of God as if they commanded a view of the Beyond, and were in possession of knowledge about the inner life of God, they also assure us that all notions fail when applied to Him, that He is beyond the grasp of the human mind and inaccessible to meditation.[25] He is the *En Sof,* the Infinite, "the most Hidden of all Hidden."[26] While there is an abysmal distance between Him and the world, He is also called All. "For all things are in Him and He is in all things … He is both manifest and concealed. Manifest in order to uphold the all and concealed, for He is found nowhere. When He becomes manifest He projects nine brilliant lights that throw light in all directions. So, too, does a lamp throw brilliance in all directions, but when we approach the brilliance we find there is nothing outside the lamp. So is the Holy ancient One, the Light of all Lights, the most Hidden of all Hidden. We can only find the light which He spreads and which appears and disappears. This light is called the Holy Name, and therefore All is One."[27]

Thus, the "Most Recondite One Who is beyond cognition does reveal of Himself a tenuous and veiled brightness shining only along a narrow path which extends from Him. This is the brightness that irradiates all."[28] The *En Sof* has granted us manifestations of His hidden life: He had descended to become the universe; He has revealed Himself to become the Lord of Israel. The ways in which the Infinite assumes the form of finite existence are called *Sefirot*.[29] These are various aspects or forms of Divine action, spheres of Divine emanation. They are, as it were, the garments in which the Hidden God reveals Himself and acts in the universe, the channels through which His light is issued forth.

The names of the ten *Sefirot are Keter Hokmah, Binah, Hesed, Geburah, Tiferet, Netsah, Hod, Yesod, Malkut*. The transition from Divine latency to activity takes place in *Keter*, the "supreme crown" of God. This stage is inconceivable, absolute unity and beyond description. In the following *Sefirot, Hogmah* and *Binahy* the building and creation of the cosmos as well as that which divides things begins. They are parallel emanations from *Ketery* representing the active and the receptive principle.

While the first triad represents the transition from the Divine to the spiritual reality, the second triad is the source of the moral order. *Hesed* stands for the love of God; *Geburah* for the power of justice manifested as severity or punishment. From the union of these emanates *Tijerety* compassion or beauty of God, mediating between *Hesed* and *Geburah*, between the life-giving power and the contrary power, holding in check what would otherwise prove to be the excesses of love.

The next triad is the source of the psychic and physical existences—*Netsah* is the lasting endurance of God, *Hod* His majesty, and *Yesod* the stability of the universe, the seat of life and vitality. *Malkut* is the kingdom, the presence of the Divine in the world. It is not a source of its own but the outflow of the other *Sefirot*, "of itself lightless, it looks up to the others and reflects them as a lamp reflects the sun."[30] It is the point at which the external world comes in contact with the upper spheres, the final manifestations of the Divine, the *Shekinah,* "the Mother of all Living."[31]

The recondite and unapproachable Self of God is usually thought of as transcendent to the *Sefirot.* There is only a diffusion of His light into the *Sefirot.* The *En Sof* and the realm of His manifestations are "linked together like the flame and the coal," the flame being a manifestation of what is latent in the coal. In the process of the emanation, the transition from the Divine to the spiritual, from the spiritual to the moral, from the moral to the physical, reality takes place. The product of this manifestation is not only the visible universe but an endless number of spiritual worlds which exist beyond the physical universe in which we live. These worlds, the hidden cosmos, constitute a most complex structure, divided into various grades and forms which can only be described in symbols. These symbols are found in the Torah, which is the constitution of the cosmos. Every letter, word or phrase in the Bible not only describes an event in the history of our world but also represents a symbol of some stage in the hidden cosmos. These are the so-called *Raze Torah,* the mysteries, that can be discovered by the mystical method of interpretation.

The system of *Sefirot* can be visualized as a tree or a man or a circle, in three triads or in three columns. According to the last image the *Sefirot* are divided into a *right* column, signifying Mercy, or light, a *left* column, signifying Severity, the absence of light, and a *central* column, signifying the synthesis of the right and left. Each *Sefirah* is a world in itself, dynamic and full of complicated mutual relations with other *Sefirot.* There are many symbols by which each *Sefirah* can be expressed, e.g., the second triad is symbolized in the lives of each of the three Patriarchs. The doctrine of *Sefirot* enables the cabbalists to perceive the bearings of God upon this world, to identify the Divine substance of all objects and events. It offers the principles by means of which all things and events can be interpreted as Divine manifestations.

The various parts of the day represent various aspects of Divine manifestation. "From sunrise until the sun declines westward it is called 'day,' and the attribute of Mercy is in the ascendant; after that it is called 'evening,' which is the time for the attribute of Severity … It is for this reason that Isaac instituted the afternoon prayer (*Minhah*), namely, to mitigate the severity of the approaching evening, whereas Abraham instituted morning prayer, corresponding to the attribute of mercy."[32]

The plurality into which the one Divine manifestation is split symbolizes the state of imperfection into which God's relation to the world was thrown. Every good deed serves to restore the original unity of the *Sefirot*, while on the other hand, "Sinners impair the supernal world by causing a separation between the 'Right' and the 'Left.' They really cause harm only to themselves, … as they prevent the descent of blessings from above … and the heaven keeps the blessings to itself." Thus the sinners' separation of the good inclination from the evil one by consciously cleaving to evil separates, as it were, the Divine attribute of Grace from that of Judgment, the Right from the Left.[33]

The Doctrine of the Shekinah

4

Originally there was harmony between God and His final manifestations, between the upper *Sefirot* and the tenth *Sefirah*. All things were attached to God and His power surged unhampered throughout all stages of being. Following the trespass of Adam, however, barriers evolved thwarting the emanation of His power. The creature became detached from the Creator, the fruit from the tree, the tree of knowledge from the tree of life, the male from the female, our universe from the world of unity, even the *Shekinah* or the tenth *Sefirah* from the upper *Sefirot*. Owing to that separation the world was thrown into disorder, the power of strict judgment increased, the power of love diminished and the forces of evil released. Man who was to exist in pure spiritual form as light in constant communication with the Divine was sunk into his present inferior state.

In spite of this separation, however, God has not withdrawn entirely from this world. Metaphorically, when Adam was driven out of Eden, an aspect of the Divine, the *Shekinah*, followed him into captivity.[34] Thus there is a Divine power that dwells in this world. It is the Divine Presence that went before Israel while they were going through the wilderness, that protects the virtuous man, that abides in his house and goes forth with him on his journeys, that dwells between a man and his wife.[35] The *Shekinah* "continually accompanies a man and leaves him not so long as he keeps the precepts of the Torah. Hence a man should be careful not to go on the road alone, that is to say, he should diligently keep the precepts of the Torah in order that he may not be deserted by the *Sheki-nah*, and so be forced to go alone without the accompaniment of the *Shekinah*."[36] The *Shekinah* follows Israel into exile and "always hovers over Israel like a mother over her children."[37] Moreover, it is because of Israel and its observance of the Torah that the *Shekinah* dwells on earth. Were they to corrupt their way, they would thrust the *Shekinah* out of this world and the earth would be left in a degenerate state.[38]

The doctrine of the *Shekinah* occupies a central place in the cabbala. While emphasizing that in His essence "the Holy One and the *Shekinah* are One,"[39] it speaks of a cleavage, as it were, in the reality of the Divine. The *Shekinah* is called figuratively the *Matrona* (symbolized by the Divine Name *Elohim*) that is separated from the King (symbolized by the ineffable Name *Has hem*) and it signifies that God is, so to speak, involved in the tragic state of this world. In the light of this doctrine the suffering of Israel assumed new meaning. Not only Israel but the whole universe, even the *Shekinah*, "lies in dust"[40] and is in exile. Man's task is to bring about the restitution of the original state of the universe and the reunion of the *Shekinah* and the En Sof. This is the meaning of Messianic salvation, the goal of all efforts.

"In time to come God will restore the *Shekinah* to its place and there will be a complete union. 'In that day shall the Lord be One and His Name One' (Zech. 14:9). It may be said: Is He not now One? no; for now through sinners He is not really One. For the Matrona is removed from the King … and the King without the Matrona is not invested with His crown as before. But when He joins the Matrona, who crowns Him with many resplendent crowns, then the supernal Mother will also crown Him in a fitting manner. But now that the King is not with the Matrona, the supernal Mother keeps her crowns and withholds from Him the waters of the stream and He is not joined with her. Therefore, as it were, He is not one. But when the Matrona shall return to the place of the Temple and the King shall be wedded with her, then all will be joined together, without separation and regarding this it is written, 'In that day shall the Lord be One and His Name One.' Then there shall be such perfection in the world as had not been for all generations before, for then shall be completeness above and below, and all worlds shall be united in one bond."[41]

The restoration of unity is a constant process. It takes place through the study of the Torah, through prayer and through the fulfillment of the commandments. "The only aim and object of the Holy One in sending man into this world is that he may know and understand that *Hashem* (God), signifying the *En Sof,* is *Elohim* (*Shekinah*). This is the sum of the whole mystery of the faith, of the whole Torah, of all that is above and below, of the written and the oral Torah, all together forming one unity."[42] "When a man sins it is as though he strips the *Shekinah* of her vestments, and that is why he is punished; and when he carries out the precepts of the law, it is as though he clothes the *Shekinah* in her vestments. Hence we say that the fringes worn by the Israelites are, to the *Shekinah* in captivity, like the poor man's garments of which it is said, 'For that is his only covering, it is his garment for his skin, wherein he shall sleep.'"[43]

MYSTIC EXPERIENCE

5

The ultimate goal of the cabbalist is not his own union with the Absolute but the union of all reality with God; one's own bliss is subordinated to the redemption of all: "we have to put all our being, all the members of our body, our complete devotion, into that thought so as to rise and attach ourselves to the *En Sof*, and thus achieve the oneness of the upper and lower worlds."[44]

What this service means in terms of personal living is described in the following way:

Happy is the portion of whoever can penetrate into the mysteries of his Master and become absorbed into Him, as it were. Especially does a man achieve this when he offers up his prayer to his Master in intense devotion, his will then becoming as the flame inseparable from the coal, and his mind concentrated on the unity of the lower firmaments, to unify them by means of a lower name, then on the unity of the higher firmaments, and finally on the absorption of them all into that most high firmament. Whilst a man's mouth and lips are moving, his heart and will must soar to the height of heights, so as to acknowledge the unity of the whole in virtue of the mystery of mysteries in which all ideas, all wills and all thoughts find their goal, to wit, the mystery of *En Sof*.[45]

The thirst for God is colored by the awareness of His holiness, of the endless distance that separates man from the Eternal One. Yet, he who craves for God is not only a mortal being, but also a part of the Community of Israel, that is, the bride of God, endowed with a soul that is "a part of God." Shy in using endearing terms in his own name, the Jewish mystic feels and speaks in the plural. The allegory of the Song of Songs would be impertinent as an individual utterance, but as an expression of Israel's love for God it is among the finest of all expressions. "God is the soul and spirit of all, and Israel calls Him so and says: (My soul), I desire Thee in order to cleave to Thee and I seek Thee early to find Thy favor."[46]

Israel lives in mystic union with God and the purpose of all its service is to strengthen this union: "O my dove that art in the clefts of the rock, in the covert of the cliff" (Song of Sol. 2:14). The "dove" here is the Community of Israel, which like a dove never forsakes her mate, the Holy One, blessed be He. "In the clefts of the rock": these are the students of the Torah, who have no ease in this world. "In the covert of the steep place": these are the specially pious among them, the saintly and God-fearing, from whom the Divine Presence never departs. The Holy One, blessed be He, inquires concerning them of the Community of Israel, saying, "Let me see thy countenance, let me hear thy voice, for sweet is thy voice"; "for above only the voice of those who study the Torah is heard. We have learned that the likeness of all such is graven above before the Holy One, blessed be He, Who delights Himself with them every day and watches them and that voice rises and pierces its way through all firmaments until it stands before the Holy One, blessed be He."[47]

The concepts of the cabbala cannot always be clearly defined and consistently interrelated. As the name of Jewish mysticism, "cabbala" (lit.: "received lore"), indicates, it is a tradition of wisdom, supposed to have been revealed to elect Sages in ancient times and preserved throughout the generations by an initiated few. The cabbalists accept at the outset the ideas on authority, not on the basis of analytical understanding.

Yet the lips of the teachers and the pages of the books are not the only sources of knowledge. The great cabbalists claimed to have received wisdom directly from the Beyond. Inspiration and Vision were as much a part of their life as contemplation and study. The prayer of Moses: "Show me, I pray Thee, Thy glory" (Ex. 33:18) has never died in the hearts of the cabbalists. The conception of the goal has changed but the quest for immediate cognition remained. The Merkaba-mystics, following perhaps late prophetic traditions about the mysteries of the Divine Throne, were striving to behold the celestial sphere in which the secrets of creation and man's destiny are contained. In the course of the centuries the scope of such esoteric experiences embraced a variety of objectives. The awareness of the cabbalists that the place whereon they stood was holy ground kept them mostly silent about the wonder that was granted to them. Yet we possess sufficient evidence to justify the assumption that mystic events, particularly in the form of inner experiences, of spiritual communications rather than that of sense perceptions, were elements of their living. According to old Rabbinic teachings, there have always been Sages and saints upon whom the Holy Spirit rested, to whom wisdom was communicated from heaven by a Voice, through the appearance of the spirit of Elijah or in dreams. According to the *Zohar*, God reveals to the saints "profound secrets of the Holy Name which He does not reveal to the angels."[48] The disciples of Rabbi Simeon ben Yohai are called prophets, "before whom both supernal and terrestrial beings tremble in awe."[48a] Others pray that the inspiration of the Holy Spirit should come upon them.[49] The perception of the unearthly is recorded as an ordinary feature in the life of certain Rabbis. "When R. Hamnuna the Ancient used to come out from the river on a Friday afternoon, he was wont to rest a little on the bank, and raising his eyes in gladness, he would say that he sat there in order to behold the joyous sight of the heavenly angels ascending and descending. At each arrival of the Sabbath, he said, man is caught up into the world of souls."[50] Not only may the human mind receive spiritual illuminations; the soul also may be bestowed upon higher powers. "Corresponding to the impulses of a man here are the influences which he attracts to himself from above. Should his impulse be toward holiness, he attracts to himself holiness from on high and so he becomes holy; but if this tendency is toward the side of impurity, he draws down toward himself the unclean spirit and so becomes polluted."[51]

Since the time of the prophet Joel the Jews have expected that at the end of days the Lord would "pour out His spirit upon all flesh" and all men would prophesy. In later times, it is believed, the light of that revelation of mysteries could already be perceived.

The mystics absorb even in this world "something of the odor of these secrets and mysteries."[52] Significantly, the Torah itself is conceived as a living source of inspiration, not as a fixed book. The Torah is a voice that "calls aloud" to men;[53] she calls them day by day to herself in love … "The Torah lets out a word and emerges for a little from her sheath, and then hides herself again. But she does this only for those who understand and obey her. She is like unto a beautiful and stately damsel, who is hidden in a secluded chamber of a palace and who has a lover of whom no one knows but she. Out of his love for her he constantly passes by her gate, turning his eyes toward all sides to find her. Knowing that he is always haunting the palace, what does she do? She opens a little door in her hidden palace, discloses for a moment her face to her lover, then swiftly hides it again. None but he notices it; but his heart and soul, and all that is in him are drawn to her, knowing as he does that she has revealed herself to him for a moment because she loves him. It is the same with the Torah, which reveals her hidden secrets only to those who love her. She knows that he who is wise of heart daily haunts the gates of her house. What does she do? She shows her face to him from her palace, making a sign of love to him, and straightaway returns to her hiding place again. No one understands her message save he alone, and he is drawn to her with heart and soul and all his being. Thus the Torah reveals herself momentarily in love to her lovers in order to awaken fresh love in them."[54]

THE TORAH – A MYSTIC REALITY

6

The Torah is an inexhaustible esoteric reality. To enter into its deep, hidden strata is in itself a mystic goal. The Universe is an image of the Torah and the Torah is an image of God. For the Torah is "the Holy of Holies"; "it consists entirely of the name of the Holy One, blessed be He. Every letter in it is bound up with that Name."[55]

The Torah[55a] is the main source from which man can draw the secret wisdom and power of insight into the essence of things. "It is called Torah (lit.: showing) because it shows and reveals that which is hidden and unknown; and all life from above is comprised in it and issues from it."[56] "The Torah contains all the deepest and most recondite mysteries; all sublime doctrines both disclosed and undisclosed; all essences both of the higher and the lower grades, of this world and of the world to come are to be found there."[57] The source of wisdom is accessible to all, yet only few resort to it. "How stupid are men that they take no pains to know the ways of the Almighty by which the world is maintained. What prevents them? Their stupidity, because they do not study the Torah; for if they were to study the Torah they would know the ways of the Holy One, blessed be He."[58]

The Torah has a double significance: literal and symbolic. Besides their plain, literal meaning, which is important, valid and never to be overlooked, the verses of the Torah possess an esoteric significance, "comprehensible only to the wise who are familiar with the ways of the Torah."[59] "Happy is Israel to whom was given the sublime Torah, the Torah of truth. Perdition take any-one who maintains that any narrative in the Torah comes merely to tell us a piece of history and nothing more! If that were so, the Torah would not be what it assuredly is, to wit, the supernal Law, the Law of truth. Now if it is not dignified for a king of flesh and blood to engage in common talk, much less to write it down, is it conceivable that the most high King, the Holy One, blessed be He, was short of sacred subjects with which to fill the Torah, so that He had to collect such commonplace topics as the anecdotes of Esau, and Hagar, Laban's talks to Jacob, the words of Balaam and his ass, those of Balak, and of Zimri, and such-like, and make of them a Torah? If so, why is it called the 'Law of Truth?' Why do we read 'The Law of the Lord is perfect … The testimony of the Lord is sure … The Ordinances of the Lord are true … More to be desired are they than gold, yea, than much fine gold' (Ps. 19:8–11). But assuredly each word of the Torah signifies sublime things, so that this or that narrative, besides its meaning in and for itself, throws light on the all-comprehensive Rule of the Torah."[60]

"Said R. Simeon: 'Alas for the man who regards the Torah as a mere book of tales and everyday matters! If that were so, we, even we, could compose a torah dealing with everyday affairs, and of even greater excellence. Nay, even the princes of the world possess books of greater worth which we could use as a model for compos-ing some such torah. The Torah, however, contains in all its words supernal truths and sublime mysteries. Observe the perfect balanc-ing of the upper and lower worlds. Israel here below is balanced by the angels on high, of whom it says: 'who makest thine angels into winds' (Ps. 104:4). For the angels in descending on earth put on themselves earthly garments, as otherwise they could not stay in this world, nor could the world endure them.

"Now, if thus it is with the angels, how much more so must it be with the Torah—the Torah that created them, that created all the worlds and is the means by which these are sustained. Thus had the Torah not clothed herself in garments of this world the world could not endure it. The stories of the Torah are thus only her outer garments, and whoever looks upon that garment as being Torah itself, woe to that man—such a one will have no portion in the next world. David thus said: 'Open thou mine eyes, that I may behold wondrous things out of Thy law' (Ps. 119:18), to wit, the things that are beneath the garment. Observe this. The garments worn by a man are the most visible part of him, and senseless people looking at the man do not seem to see more in him than the garments. But in truth the pride of the garments is the body of the man, and the pride of the body is the soul. Similarly the Torah has a body made up of the precepts of the Torah, called *gufe torah* (bodies, main principles of the Torah), and that body is enveloped in garments made up of worldly narratives. The senseless people only see the garment, the mere narrations; those who' are somewhat wise penetrate as far as the body. But the really wise, the servants of the most high King, those who stood on Mt. Sinai, penetrate right through to the soul, the root principle of all, namely to the real Torah. In the future the same are destined to penetrate even to the super-soul (soul of the soul) of the Torah ..."[61]

How assiduously should one ponder over each word of the Torah, for there is not a single word in it which does not contain allusions to the Supernal Holy Name, not a word which does not contain many mysteries, many aspects, many roots, many branches! Where now is this "book of the wars of the Lord"? What is meant, of course, is the Torah, for as the members of the Fellowship have pointed out, he who is engaged in the battle of the Torah, struggling to penetrate into her mysteries, will wrest from his struggles an abundance of peace.[62]

The Mystic Way of Life

7

A longing for the unearthly, a yearning for purity, the will to holiness, connected the conscience of the cabbalists with the strange current of mystic living. Being puzzled or inquisitive will not make a person mystery stricken. The cabbalists were not set upon exploring, or upon compelling the unseen to become visible. Their intention was to integrate their thoughts and deeds into the secret order, to assist God in undoing the evil, in redeeming the light that was concealed. Though working with fragile tools for a mighty end, they were sure of bringing about at the end the salvation of the universe and of this tormented world.

A new form of living was the consequence of the cabbala. Everything was so replete with symbolic significance as to make it the potential heart of the spiritual universe. How carefully must all be approached. A moral rigorism that hardly leaves any room for waste or respite resulted in making the cabbalist more meticulous in studying and fulfilling the precepts of the Torah, in refining his moral conduct, in endowing every-day actions with solemn significance. For man represents God in this world. Even the parts of his body signify Divine mysteries.

Everything a man does leaves its imprint on the world. "The Supernal Holy King does not permit anything to perish, not even the breath of the mouth. He has a place for everything, and makes it what He wills. Even a human word, yes, even the voice, is not void, but has its place and destination in the universe."[63] Every action here below, if it is done with the intention of serving the

Holy King, produces a "breath" in the world above, and there is no breath which has no voice; and this voice ascends and crowns itself in the supernal world and becomes an intercessor before the Holy One, blessed be He. Contrariwise, every action which is not done with this purpose becomes a "breath" which floats about the world, and when the soul of the doer leaves his body, this "breath" rolls about like a stone in a sling, and it "breaks the spirit." The act done and the word spoken in the service of the Holy One, however, ascend high above the sun and become a holy breath, which is the seed sown by man in that world and is called *Zedakah* (righteousness) or (loving-kindness), as it is written: "Sow to yourselves according to righteousness" (Hos. 10:12). This "breath" guides the departed soul and brings it into the region of the supernal glory, so that it is "bound in the bundle of life with the Lord thy God" (I Sam. 25:29). It is concerning this that it is written: "Thy righteousness shall go before thee; the glory of the Lord shall be thy reward" (Is. 58:8). That which is called "the glory of the Lord" gathers up the souls of that holy breath, and this is indeed ease and comfort for them; but the other is called "breaking of spirit." Blessed are the righteous whose works are "above the sun" and who sow a seed of righteousness which makes them worthy to enter the world to come.[64]

Everything a man does leaves its imprint upon the world: his breath, thought, speech. If it is evil, the air is defiled and he who comes close to that trace may be affected by it and led to do evil. By fulfilling the Divine precepts man purifies the air and turns the "evil spirits" into "holy spirits." He should strive to spiritualize the body and to make it identical with the soul by fulfilling the 248 positive and 365 negative precepts which correspond to the 248 limbs and the 365 sinews of the human body. The precepts of the Torah contain "manifold sublime recondite teachings and radiances and resplendences,"[65] and can lift man to the supreme level of existence.

The purpose of man's service is to "give strength to God," not to attain one's own individual perfection. Man is able to stir the supernal spheres. "The terrestrial world is connected with the heavenly world, as the heavenly world is connected with the terrestrial one."[66] In fulfilling the good the corresponding sphere on high is strengthened; in balking it, the sphere is weakened. This connection or correspondence can be made to operate in a creative manner by means of *kawwanah* or contemplation of the mysteries of which the words and precepts of the Torah are the symbols. In order to grasp the meaning of those words or to fulfill the purpose of those precepts one has to resort to the Divine Names and Qualities which are invested in those words and precepts, the mystic issues to which they refer, or, metaphorically, the gates of the celestial mansion which the spiritual content of their fulfillment has to enter. Thus, all deeds—study, prayer and ceremonies—have to be performed not mechanically but while meditating upon their mystic significance.

Prayer is a powerful force in this service and a venture full of peril. He who prays is a priest at the temple that is the cosmos. With good prayer he may "build worlds," with improper prayer he may "destroy worlds." "It is a miracle that a man survives the hour of worship," the Baal Shem said. "The significance of all our prayers and praises is that by means of them the upper fountain may be filled; and when it is so filled and attains completeness, then the universe below, and all that appertains thereto, is filled also and receives completeness from the completion which has been consummated in the upper sphere. The world below cannot, indeed, be in a state of harmony unless it receives that peace and perfection from above, even as the moon has no light in herself but shines with the reflected radiance of the sun. All our prayers and intercessions have this purpose, namely, that the region from whence light issues may be invigorated; for then from its reflection all below is supplied."[67] "Every word of prayer that issues from a man's mouth ascends aloft through all firmaments to a place where it is tested. If it is genuine, it is taken up before the Holy King to be fulfilled, but if not it is rejected, and an alien spirit is evoked by it."[68] For example, "it is obligatory for every Israelite to relate the story of the

Exodus on the Passover night. He who does so fervently and joyously, telling the tale with a high heart, shall be found worthy to rejoice in the *Shekinah* in the world to come, for rejoicing brings forth rejoicing; and the joy of Israel causes the Holy One Himself to be glad, so that He calls together all the Family above and says unto them: 'Come ye and hearken unto the praises which My children bring unto Me! Behold how they rejoice in My redemption!' Then all the angels and supernal beings gather round and observe Israel, how she sings and rejoices because of her Lord's own Redemption—and seeing the rejoicings below, the supernal beings also break into jubilation for that the Holy One possesses on earth a people so holy, whose joy in the Redemption of their Lord is so great and powerful. For all that terrestrial rejoicing increases the power of the Lord and His hosts in the regions above, just as an earthly king gains strength from the praises of his subjects, the fame of his glory being thus spread throughout the world."[69]

Worship came to be regarded as a pilgrimage into the supernal spheres, with the prayerbook as an itinerary, containing the course of the gradual ascent of the spirit. The essential goal of man's service is to bring about the lost unity of all that exists. To render praise unto Him is not the final purpose. "Does the God of Abraham need an exaltation? Is He not already exalted high above our comprehension? … Yet man can and must exalt Him in the sense of uniting in his mind all the attributes in the Holy Name, for this is the supremest form of worship."[70] By meditating upon the mysteries while performing the Divine precepts, we act toward unifying all the supernal potencies in one will and bringing about the union of the Master and the Matrona.

Concerning the verse in Ps. 145:18, "The Lord is nigh to all them that call upon Him, to all that call upon Him in truth," the *Zohar* remarks that the words "in truth" mean in possession of the full knowledge which enables the worshiper perfectly "to unite the letters of the Holy Name in prayer … On the achievement of that unity hangs both celestial and terrestrial worship … If a man comes to unify the Holy Name, but without proper concentration of mind and devotion of heart, to the end that the supernal and terrestrial hosts should be blessed thereby, then his prayer is rejected and all beings denounce him, and he is numbered with those of whom the Holy One said, 'When ye come to see my countenance, who hath required this from your hand, to tread my courts?' All the 'countenances' of the King are hidden in the depths of darkness, but for those who know how perfectly to unite the Holy Name, all the walls of darkness are burst asunder, and the diverse 'countenances' of the King are made manifest, and shine upon all, bringing blessing to heavenly and earthly beings."[71]

The lower things are apparent, the higher things remain unrevealed. The higher an essence is, the greater is the degree of its concealment. To pray is "to draw blessings from the depth of the 'Cistern,' from the source of all life … Prayer is the drawing of this blessing from above to below ; for when the Ancient One, the All-hidden, wishes to bless the universe, He lets His gifts of, Grace collect in that supernal depth, from whence they are to be drawn, through human prayer, into the 'Cistern,' so that all the streams and brooks may be filled therefrom." The verse in Psalm 130:1, "Out of the depths have I called Thee," is said to mean not only that he who prays should do so from the depths of his soul; he must also invoke the blessing from the source of all sources.[72]

The Concern for God

8

The yearning for mystic living, the awareness of the ubiquitous mystery, the noble nostalgia for the nameless nucleus, have rarely subsided in the Jewish soul. This longing for the mystical has found many and varied expressions in ideas and doctrines, in customs and songs, in visions and aspirations. It is a part of the heritage of the psalmists and prophets.

There were Divine commandments to fulfill, rituals to perform, laws to obey—but the psalmist did not feel as if he carried a yoke: "Thy statutes have been my songs" (119:54). The fulfillment of the *mitzvot* was felt to be not a mechanical compliance but a personal service in the palace of the King of Kings. Is mysticism alien to the spirit of Judaism? Listen to the psalmist: "As the hart panteth after the water brooks, so panteth my soul after Thee, O Lord. My soul thirsteth for God, for the Living God; when shall I come and appear before God?" (42:2–3). "My soul yearneth, yea even pineth for the courts of the Lord; my heart and my flesh sing for joy unto the Living God" (84:3). "For a day in Thy courts is better than a thousand" (84:11). "In Thy presence is fulness of joy" (16:11).

It has often been said that Judaism is an earthly religion, yet the psalmist states, "I am a sojourner in the earth" (119:19). "Whom have I in heaven but Thee? And beside thee I desire none upon earth" (73:25). "My flesh and my heart faileth; but God is the rock of my heart and my portion forever" (73:26). "But as for me, the nearness of God is my good" (73:28). "O God, Thou art my God;

earnestly will I seek Thee; my soul thirsteth for Thee, my flesh longeth for Thee in a dry and weary land, where no water is … for Thy lovingkindness is better than life. My soul is satisfied as with marrow and fatness; … I remember Thee upon my couch and meditate on Thee in the nightwatches … My soul cleaveth unto Thee, Thy right hand holdeth me fast" (63:2, 4, 6, 7, 9).

In their efforts to say what God is and wills, the prophets sought to imbue Israel with two impulses: to realize that God is holy, different and apart from all that exists, and to bring into man's focus the dynamics that prevail between God and man. The first impulse placed the mind in the restful light of the knowledge of unity, omnipotence, and superiority of God to all other beings, while the second impulse turned the hearts toward the inexhaustible heavens of God's concern for man, at times brightened by His mercy, at times darkened by His anger. He is both transcendent, beyond human understanding, and at the same time full of love, compassion, grief, or anger. The prophets did not intend to afford man a view of heaven, to report about secret things they saw and heard but to disclose what happened in God in reference to Israel. What they preached was more than a concept of Divine might and wisdom. They spoke of an inner life of God, of His love or anger, His mercy or disappointment, His interest or participation in the fate of Israel and other nations. God revealed Himself to the prophets in a specific state, in an emotional or passionate relationship to Israel. He not only demanded obedience but He was personally concerned and even stirred by the conduct of His people. Their actions aroused His joy, grief or disappointment. His attitude was not objective but subjective. He was not only a Judge but also a Father. He is the lover, engaged to His people, who reacts to human life with a specific *pathos*, signified in the language of the prophets, in love, mercy or anger. The Divine pathos which the prophets tried to express in many ways was not a name for His essence but rather for the modes of this reaction to Israel's conduct which could be changed by a change in Israel's conduct. Such a change was often the object of the prophetic ministry.

The prophets discovered the holy dimension of living by which our right to live and to survive is measured. However, the holy dimension was not a mechanical magnitude, measurable by the yardstick of deed and reward, of crime and punishment, by a cold law of justice. They did not proclaim a universal moral mechanism but a spiritual order in which justice was the course but not the source. To them justice was not a static principle but a surge sweeping from the inwardness of God, in which the deeds of man find, as it were, approval or disapproval, joy or sorrow. There was a surge of Divine pathos, which came to the souls of the prophets like a fierce passion, startling, shaking, burning, and led them forth to the perilous defiance of people's self-assurance and contentment. Beneath all songs and sermons they held conference with God's concern for the people, with the well out of which the tides of anger raged.

There is always a correspondence between what man is and what he knows about God. To a man of the *vita actwa*, omnipotence is the most striking attribute of God. A man with an inner life, to whom thoughts and intuitions are not less real than things and deeds, will search for a concept of the inner life of God. The concept of inner life in the Divine Being is an idea upon which the mystic doctrines of Judaism hinge. The significance of prophetic revelation lies not in the inner experience of the prophet but in its character as a manifestation of what is in God. Prophetic revelation is primarily an event in the life of God. This is the outstanding difference between prophetic revelation and all other types of inspiration as reported by many mystics and poets. To the prophet it is not a psychic event, but first of all a transcendent act, something that happens to God. The actual reality of revelation takes place outside the consciousness of the prophet. He experiences revelation, so to speak, as an ecstasy of God, who comes out of His imperceivable distance to reveal His will to man. Essentially, the act of revelation takes place in the Beyond; it is merely directed upon the prophet.

The knowledge about the inner state of the Divine in its relationship to Israel determined the inner life of the prophets, engendering a passion for God, a *sympathy* for the Divine pathos in their hearts. They loved Israel because God loved Israel, and they frowned upon Israel when they knew that such was the attitude of God. Thus the marriage of Hosea was an act of sympathy; the prophet had to go through the experience of being betrayed as Israel had betrayed God. He had to experience in his own life what it meant to be betrayed by a person whom he loved in order to gain an understanding of the inner life of God. In a similar way the sympathy for God was in the heart of Jeremiah like a "burning fire, shut up in my bones and I weary myself to hold it in, but cannot" (20:9).

The main doctrine of the prophets can be called *pathetic theology*. Their attitude toward what they knew about God can be described as religion of sympathy. The Divine pathos, or as it was later called, the *Middot*, stood in the center of their consciousness. The life of the prophet revolved around the life of God. The prophets were not indifferent to whether God was in a state of anger or a state of mercy. They were most sensitive to what was going on in God.[73]

This is the pattern of Jewish mysticism: to have an open heart for the inner life of God. It is based on two assumptions: that there is an inner life in God and that the existence of man ought to revolve in a spiritual dynamic course around the life of God.[73a]

Notes

1   *Zohar* (to which all unspecified references in the following notes relate. The translation used is that mentioned in the Bibliography.) II, 23a.

2   I 241a.

3   II 15b.

4   II 20a.

5   I 156b.

6   I 2a.

7   II 15b.

7a   III 128a.

8   Cf. *Midrash Rabbah* (Soncino Press Edition. London, 1939), Gen. XVII; Mid. Hag. Gn. 2, 7.

9   *Pesik*, ed. Buber, XXVI, 166b.

10   III 65b.

11   Gen. R., *op. cit.,* LXIX. 35 Cf. Louis Ginzberg, *Cabala*, JE, v. 3.

12   Gen. R., *op. cit.,* XLVII. 6; LXXXII, 6.

13   II 75a.

14   II 76a.

15   II 23b.

16   II 12a.

17   II 144a.

18   I 164a.

19   III 92a–92b.

20   III 64b.

21   II 1433a.

22   III 64a.

23   II 220b.

24   III 109b.

25   II 42b.

26   I 21a.

27   III 288a.

28   II 146b.

29   *Tikkune Zohar*, 1.

30   II 23a; cf. I, 27a; II 158a.

31   On the concept of *Shekinah* in rabbinic literature cf. J. Abelson, *The Immanence of God in Rabbinical Literature*. London, 1912.

32   II 22a–21b.

33   II 26b.

34   I 22b.

35   I 76a.

36   I 230a.

37   II 120b.

38   I 61a.

39   II 118b.

40   II 9b.

41   III 77b.

42   II 161b.

43   I 23b.

44   II 216a–b.

45   II 213b.

46   III 67a.

47   III 61a.

48   III 78b.

48   a II 144b.

49   II 154a.

50   II 136b.

51   I 125b; cf. I 99b.

52   *Sefer Hassidin*, ed. Wistinetzki (Frankfort, 1924). Cf. *Zohar* I 105b.

53   III 58a; III 23a.

54   II 99a.

55   III 73a.

[55a Cf. Robert Gordis, "The Bible as a Cultural Monument," see also Louis Finkelstein, "The Jewish Religion: Its Beliefs and Practices," both published in "The Jews, Their History, Culture and Religion" 2 vols., editor Louis Finkelstein, Harpers, 1949, New York.]

56   III 53b.

57   I 134b–135a.

58   III 75b.

59   II 95a.

60   III 52a.

61   III 152a.

62   III 55b–56a.

63   II 100b.

64   III 59a.

65   II 218b.

66   I 70b.

67   II 1045b.

68   III 55a.

69   III 40b.

70   II 55b.

71   II 57a.

72   III 63a.

73   Cf. Abraham Heschel, *Die Prophetie* (Cracow, 1936), pp. 56–87; 127–180.

[73a For the influence of cabbala on the philosophic thought of the Renaissance see below Alexander Altmann, "Judaism and World Philosophy," in "The Jews, Their History, Culture and Religion" 2 vols., editor Louis Finkelstein, Harpers, 1949, New York, pp. 650–651.]

BIBLIOGRAPHY

Only an inkling of the vast literature of Jewish mysticism can be offered in the limits of a single chapter. It was considered proper to dwell primarily upon one phase of the Cabbala, the history of which abounds in thoughts and events. The *Zohar*, the authoritative book of the movement, was chosen as the basis of our chapter.

GINZBERG, LOUIS
Cabala," in *The Jewish Encyclopedia*, III, 456–479. New York and London, 1902.

SCHOLEM, GERHARD G.
Major Trends in Jewish Mysticism. Jerusalem, 1941.

WAITE, ARTHUR E.
The Holy Kabbalah. London, 1929.
The Zohar. Translated by Harry Sperling and Maurice Simon. 4 vols. London, 1931–1934.

Made in the USA
Middletown, DE
24 December 2022